49

MW00764724

TEAMWORK SKILLS

THE CAREER SKILLS LIBRARY

Communication Skills
By Richard Worth

Information Management
By Joseph Mackall

Leadership Skills
By Diane E. Rossiter

Learning the Ropes
By Sharon Naylor

Organization Skills
By Richard Worth

Problem-Solving
By Dandi Daiey Mackall

Self-Development
By Dandi Daley Mackall

Teamwork Skills
By Dandi Daley Mackall

TEAMWORK SKILLS

by Dandi Daley Mackall

A New England Publishing Associates Book

Printed in the United States of America
U-8

Library of Congress Cataloging-in-Publication Data

Mackall, Dandi Daley.
   Teamwork skills / by Dandi Daley Mackall
      p. cm.
   Includes bibliographical references and index.
   Summary: Examines the interpersonal skills that help individuals to be successful on the job.
   ISBN 0-89434-212-6
   1. Teams in the workplace. [1. Teams in the workplace. 2. Interpersonal relations.] I. Title
   HD66.M325   1998
   658.4'02—dc21   97-26632
                                      CIP
                                      AC

4

CONTENTS

INTRODUCTION

Most of us have been part of a team. Your family acts as a team, dividing the labor, working out relationships. In school, sooner or later you're bound to end up on a group project. You might play sports, participate in the band, sing in a choir, cheer on a squad, or serve on a student committee.

You know how teams work...and how they don't.

Most corporations and businesses believe in the effectiveness of workplace teams. Millions of dollars are spent each year training employees to work together and get along. Why? Because teams work. They produce greater profits and more satisfied employees.

Teams work. They produce greater profits and more satisfied employees.

FACTOID:

Charles Schwab claimed industrialist Andrew Carnegie paid him a million dollars a year—not for his intelligence or knowledge of steel—but because of Schwab's ability to get along with people.

How are you at getting along with people? Each year thousands of highly skilled people and former A-students fail to fit into corporate teams. Their individual skills are strong, but they can't function as part of a team. And in the modern workforce, only people with strong team skills will be able to make it. Those without these skills will find themselves looking for another job.

Lee Wilkins, manager of human resources for the Gorman-Rupp Company, an international manufacturing firm, puts it this way: "We can teach new hires the job skills they need to succeed. What we can't teach is how to fit in and get along with the rest of the team. And if they can't do that, they'll never make it."

WHY "DREAM DRAFT PICKS" FAIL TO MAKE CORPORATE DREAM TEAMS

1. Can't work as part of a team
2. Poor people skills
3. Poor communication skills
4. Inability to learn and flex
5. Don't carry their weight
6. Lack of dedication to the corporate team
7. Negative attitude
8. Won't learn from teammates
9. Personality conflicts
10. Selfishness

If you want to succeed in the workplace, you'll need to know how to work with a team. And if you think it's tough getting along with your algebra classmates, wait till you join the fast-paced, multicultural business world!

And even if you *do* survive your probation period with the corporate dream team, you're still not off the hook. Now, you have to *keep* your position. Few workers stick with the same job for 20 years anymore. Jobs and technical skills change as industry changes. We switch jobs or our jobs change. People skills are what keep talented people employed.

"...our military forces are one team—in the game to win regardless of who carries the ball. This is no time for 'fancy dans' who won't hit the line with all they have on every play, unless they can call the signals. Each player on this team—whether he shines in the spotlight of the backfield or eats dirt in the line—must be an All-American."
—Omar Bradley

In this book we'll take a close look at corporate teams and the kinds of employees they're seeking.

CHAPTER ONE
THE CORPORATE DREAM TEAM

WHY TEAMS?

When the U.S. Women's Olympic softball team met in Atlanta for the 1996 Olympics, most sportswriters didn't give them a chance at the gold. Who were these women anyway? Thirty-four-year-old shortstop Dot Richardson had to take time off from practicing surgery to join the team. Pitcher Michele Smith had been in Japan for five years, teaching English to Toyota employees. Another team member, Sheila Cornell, had just received her master's in physical therapy from the University of Southern California and was looking for a job "reading books all day."

But these individuals came together to form something magical, a greatness none could have achieved on her own. They practiced, drilled, sacrificed, and kept each other going through 64 games in the two months before Atlanta. These women became a team, an unstoppable force, and brought home Olympic gold medals.

(Courtesy: U.S.A. Softball)

Strong team skills are important in the workplace today. As an individual, you may have many talents, but when you become part of a group to achieve a common goal, only teamwork can ensure success. That's what enabled the U.S. Women's softball team to win the gold at the 1996 Olympic Games in Atlanta.

When a poor boy named Sam came up with an idea for full-scale discount operations in small towns, few people listened. Sam had a vision for an organization in which employees considered themselves a family, part of the team.

Sam worked in other people's stores until he could beg and borrow enough money to open his own. He encouraged suggestions from his employees and put

(Courtesy: Wal-Mart Stores, Inc.)

Sam M. Walton, founder of Wal-Mart Stores, encouraged his employees to work together as a family unit. His emphasis on teamwork made Wal-Mart one of the most successful corporations in the world.

their ideas to good use. His business grew, and Sam opened other stores. He visited each "team" regularly. Several mornings a week Sam could be found sitting on a crate or standing in front of a crowd of employees and leading the company cheer: "Give me a W! Give me an A! Give me an L! Give me an M! Give me an A! Give me an R! Give me a T!"

When Sam Walton died in 1992, he left a fortune of $2.5 billion and 1,720 Wal-Mart stores spread across the United States. Most biographers credit Walton's success in large measure to his unique ability to make his employees feel like a family and operate like a team.

Small teams are becoming the basic unit of corporate organization. Why are major corporations using teams to get the job done? Because teams work.

> Small teams are becoming the basic unit of corporate organization.

F A C T O I D :
Even animals are into teamwork. When geese fly in the "V" formation, they can travel 70% faster than when they fly alone.

WHY ME?

You make it to your dream job. You feel you've arrived. Confident it was your unsurpassed skills that brought you such success, you report for work. It's your first day at your new job, and you're ready to take on the world single-handedly.

You do your best, strut your stuff. For 90 days you come up with ideas to increase your company's profits. Each week you make sure your brilliance shines. Your reports have to be better than anyone else's.

After three months, you're ready for your first evaluation. Confident of your personal success, you march into the boss's office.

"Sorry," your boss begins. "It doesn't appear to be working out for you as we'd hoped. You're just not cut out for our team here. I'm afraid we're going to have to let you go."

You've been cut from the corporate dream team.

The scene happens over and over, usually within the first 90 days of a new career. The battle isn't over once you've landed your dream job. You have to prove yourself. You have to earn your place on your team by fitting in.

One executive, who has managed over a dozen businesses on the East Coast, put it this way: "The ability to get along with people doesn't just come in handy. You won't survive without it. Somebody said it was a jungle out there? Ha! Compared to what's

The battle isn't over once you've landed your dream job.

(Joe Duffy)

really waiting out there in the world of high finance, jungles are for wimps."

It will be up to you to prove you can work as part of a team. *Teamwork.*

TEAMS=Together Each Accomplishes More Success!

> —from James Lundy's Teams:
> *How to Develop Peak Performance*
> *Teams for World Class Results*

16

TEAMWORK! TEAMWORK! TEAMWORK!

So what is it? Teamwork is the process of a group of people pooling their resources and skills to work together and achieve a common goal. In other words, your boss will be looking for two things from his dream team: *team* and *work.*

PUTTING THE "TEAM" IN TEAMWORK

Your mother told you first. Try to get along with people. Make friends. Play nice. Share.

Now you're in the big leagues. You can't just pick up your bat and go home anymore. Stakes are high, often in the millions of dollars. One Chicago stockbroker, fully aware of the high stakes in the business world, said: "This company could lose more money in 60 seconds than I could make in 60 years. Nothing I do ends with me. We're in this together."

No matter how skilled or talented you may be, if you can't get along with other members of your team, you won't last long.

Kala

Kala learned about teams the hard way. She received three job offers before she finished her senior year at Oklahoma University. After interviews and sleepless

(V. Harlow)

As youngsters, we all learn the basic rules of life, such as being nice to people and sharing. Continue to practice these rules and you'll achieve success in the workplace.

nights, she decided on an entry-level position at Estee Lauder. She liked the hours and the promise of rapid advancement to management levels.

Her first duties threw her into perfume sales in a posh department store. Kala was disappointed with her co-workers. For one thing, they were older than her recruiter had led her to expect. Kala missed her college friends. *These* women hadn't even attended college.

But no matter. Kala saw her job on the department store floor as a jumping-off point. She'd show them what she could do, and move on fast.

Life didn't work out that way. Kala's team seemed to read her thoughts. They didn't like being used as a "step" on someone else's career ladder. On every break, Kala left the department instead of trying to get to know her coworkers. Her team resented Kala's inattention to detail. They sensed her lack of interest in any part of the business that didn't directly affect her.

A year later, Kala reflects on her first weeks at Estee Lauder. "I couldn't believe the people I worked with didn't like me. In college, I could get along with any-body. So I figured it must be their fault. They resented me because I was making more sales than they were. I just wanted to do my job and move on."

But when Kala's three-month trial period ended, she was in for a shock. "I was expecting praise and rewards for all the sales I made. But the whole evalu-ation sounded lukewarm. And the biggest notation said: 'Not a team player!' I couldn't believe it. I don't know if I was more surprised that someone would say I wasn't a team player—or more shocked that man-agement would care so much. I left the company before they could fire me."

Companies do care about teams. Experts advise that teamwork can improve productivity 10% to 40%. Teams in the workplace are expected to be more than the sum of individual members. That means team members may have to spend as much energy working at team relationships as they will getting the job done.

Experts advise that teamwork can improve productivity 10% to 40%.

Workers need interpersonal team skills that will enable them to fit in. Jerry Richmond managed chain stores for Sears and Woolworth before owning his own retail business. He says, "I've seen talented people come and go. But my advice for students is: The best skill you can develop is to get along with people. Cooperation with your team covers a multitude of sins."

TEAM...WHAT?

Developing good team skills will help prepare you for working with a group of people. You should come to think of your coworkers as a team, whether or not your company officially designates team units.

But forming a team is only part of the picture. You can't forget the second half of *teamwork: work.* If you forget the *work* in *teamwork,* you may end up with some nice friends...who can go job hunting with you. Companies expect teams to produce.

A saying that goes around Goldman Sachs Banking, an investment bank, is, "Corporations pay for performance, not for potential."

Interpersonal skills are essential. But teamwork is more than getting along with others. Your new employer will expect your team to work. You'll have to get the job done. Together, you will need to tackle problems, complete tasks—work.

Larry

Fortunately, when Larry joined a California team of researchers, he took with him a school experience in teamwork. In junior high, Larry and four friends formed an extracurricular group to compete in Odyssey of the Mind, a science competition. Their task was spelled out for them. Each team had to demonstrate a scientific principle through a physical representation.

In certain ways, Larry and his friends made a great team. They got along well, joked, encouraged each other. Larry wasn't sold on his buddy's idea to build a paper mache volcano. He knew it lacked originality. But Larry didn't want to hurt his friend's feelings, so he went along.

Larry looked forward to their meetings. Everybody had a great time. Not much work got accomplished.

(V Harlow/Vinal Recional Vocational Technical School, Middletown, CT)

Learning basic team skills while you're in high school will help you when you start your first job. You'll accomplish your goals more quickly and easily when you have a good relationship with other members of the group.

But between the gossip and refreshments, the team managed to throw together a volcano that erupted on command.

In the end, however, Larry's team bombed. They placed next to last in the competition. They thought they knew what it meant to be a good team. But Larry admits his group of friends had no idea what teamwork required.

TAKING IT WITH YOU

Larry took his school team experience with him to his first job. For the last year, Larry has been part of a research development team. He's discovered that good relationships are necessary. But that's not all there is to it.

Referring to his research team, Larry explains: "At first, before we knew each other, it seemed like we got more work done. We each did our own thing and kept out of each other's way. Then when we got to know and like each other, it was harder to get anything done. We had a great time together. But we weren't getting anywhere. It reminded me of my old Odyssey of the Mind group."

But Larry had learned from his mistakes. With his Odyssey of the Mind buddies, he hadn't wanted to risk damaging friendships just to get the job done. This time, he wanted friends, but he knew they *had* to get the job done.

Larry talked to his team about the problem. Finally, they began to focus on their goals. Team members made compromises and the team started to find its way. They plowed through and discovered they could accomplish their goals if they made themselves and each other accountable for the work.

"And that," Larry says, "is when we started working together as a team."

Later, in Larry's first-year evaluation with his supervisor, he discovered how vital teamwork was to his employers. The work his team accomplished together weighed more heavily in the evaluation than anything Larry had done on his own.

TEAMWORK BAGGAGE

As you leave school and head for your new job, take some time to assess the teamwork skills you practiced while you were a student. There are certain skills you'll want to take with you, and others you'll need to leave behind.

TEAMWORK SKILLS TO...

Take Along	**Leave Behind**
Personal responsibility	Personal glory
Ability to motivate the team	"Star" mentality
Constructive competitive spirit	Destructive competitive spirit
Ability to look like your team	Old school uniform
Ability to laugh at yourself	Locker-room jokes
Ability to please your new boss	Your old coach's ways of doing things

---

F A C T O I D :

When Chrysler decided to create a sports car to compete with the Corvette, the company brought together a team of over 40 of their brightest employees. The result was the Dodge Viper, a $54,000 car that could go 160 mph. It gave Chrysler a much-needed image boost.

Teams work. Employers believe in the power of teams. That's why businesses look for people with good team skills. You may think you've got it made once you pass that interview and get that job offer. But you haven't. You're on probation. And it's not merely a case of what your boss thinks about you. Your people skills have to work on your entire work team.

If you want a spot on the corporate dream team, you may have to change your ideas about what makes a dream player. Paul Kaponya, a management consultant for a variety of leading corporations, said: "Experience and validated studies indicate that the single most important factor affecting success and failure is the ability to work effectively with others."

Want to make it in the majors? Teamwork. Teamwork. Teamwork.

EXERCISE

1. Make up your own definition of teamwork.

2. List all the "teams" of which you've been a part. Which of these teams worked best? Why do you think that team succeeded?

2 CHAPTER TWO
GET SMART: GET PEOPLE SMART

Here lies one who knew how to get around
him men who were cleverer than himself.
—Andrew Carnegie's self-written epithet

Christine and Beth beat out a tough crowd of applicants to join an established, Texas-based investment firm. Beth had stronger computer skills than Christine and also brought along a little experience in sales. Although their educational backgrounds were similar, Beth made better grades in college.

Yet a year later, Christine found herself on the fast track to success. Beth still had her job, but she was looking for a new one. She knew she'd never get anywhere in the firm, and her supervisor agreed.

What happened? Why did Christine succeed her first year on the job, but Beth—with her stronger skills—didn't?

One of the members on Christine's and Beth's team confided, "I knew from that first week which one would make it. Christine was people-smart. Beth wasn't. It's as simple as that."

Business guru Gordon Wainwright says, "Your success in your organization will depend in large measure on how well you deal with the other people in it."

"Your success in your organization will depend in large measure on how well you deal with the other people in it."

PLAYING DETECTIVE

Now that you know how vital being a team member is...Now that you're convinced if the team doesn't buy into you, you're out...what can you do about it?

Become a detective. Discover all you can about your coworkers so you can build strong working relationships. Can you read between the lines as people talk? Can you decipher body language when they're silent? Do you have a feeling for who likes to be left alone and who's offended when you don't include him?

FACTOID:

The U.S. Secretary of Labor's Commission on Achieving Necessary Skills (SCANS) defines interpersonal skills as "the ability to work on teams, teach others, serve customers, lead, negotiate, and work well with people from different cultural backgrounds."

28

Imagine it's your first day at your new job. Your team (Rachel, Missy, Bruno, and Slick) heads for lunch. You tag along...and observe.

The five of you take your seats around the linen-covered table, Rachel taking the unofficial head. Poor Missy loses her balance as Slick brushes her aside and takes a seat next to Rachel. Missy moves silently, eyes down, and sits stiffly next to Slick. You take the chair across from Missy as Bruno plops between you and Rachel.

"I'm sick of this place," Bruno says. He picks up the menu, glances at it, and snaps it shut. Sighing deeply, he leans back, one arm over the back of his chair.

Missy hasn't looked up from her menu.

"What are you having, Rachel?" Slick asks, sipping his water. It doesn't appear that he's reading his own menu.

Rachel carefully closes her menu, greets the people at the adjacent table. She speaks to you, rather than answering Slick directly. "The fish is quite good here. So's the salad and the veal."

Bruno grunts. His eyes roll toward the ceiling.

The waiter comes and starts with Missy. "Madame?" he says.

Missy's eyes peek over the top of the menu. "Umm, I'll take the...." She straightens her back even more and tugs on the collar of her suit jacket. "Would you please come back to me?" she asks softly.

"Fish," Slick says, his teeth shining like a shark's. "And salad."

Rachel orders. "I'll have the veal, crisp salad with light dressing on the side, iced tea, no sugar, baked potato with light sour cream on the side and no butter. Thank you."

Bruno orders spaghetti and warns the waiter not to overcook it this time and to bring him extra garlic bread. He shakes his head at your order.

Missy swallows hard. "I guess I'll have the same," she says, motioning to you, but not looking at you.

Then you wait for your food. And you keep on observing.

Play detective. What could you learn about your team members? For example, Rachel is at least the unofficial leader, commanding deference from the others. She is probably orderly, organized, possibly someone to keep your eye on as a mentor. She knows how to network (greeting others at the adjacent table), and she knows what she wants. It would probably be worth your time to understand what she expects from you on the job. To earn her respect, you'll have to be organized and efficient.

Slick may be someone you'll have to look out for. Watch him to see if he's willing to do anything to look good to the higher-ups. Unfortunately, there are a lot of "Slicks" out there. If you're a good detective, you'll know when to watch your back.

Bruno is the kind of guy who will likely criticize everything you do. You can learn to get along with him, but don't expect him to encourage you on the job. Be careful not to get caught up in his negativism. You may not want to be labeled as belonging to Bruno's camp.

Obviously Missy appears shy and weak. But don't write her off. Never write off anybody on your team. Think of ways you can encourage quiet members. Ask her questions in her area of expertise. Ask for her opinion. You may be surprised at what she has to offer. And you may be the one who can help her realize her potential and become more effective on the team.

The more you know about the members of the team, the better chance you'll have for a smooth transition and good team relationships. You don't need to box everybody into categories your first week, but an idea of each member's personality type, learning style and role can help you understand the dynamics of your team.

ACCEPTING TEAM MEMBERS

Although you may think that your way is the right way, you're not on your team to change your teammates. You're there to learn how best to work with them and achieve team goals.

So what do you do when you meet a "Bruno"? You accept him. Instead of trying to change his behavior, adapt your own. Anticipate his behavior based on how you've seen him act in other situations. Don't let him take you by surprise. Be prepared. When you ask for his input, don't expect a compliment. Brace yourself for criticism. Pick out any parts of his critique that will help your performance, and let the rest roll off you. You know his nature. That's okay. He may have said something you can use.

People can sense when someone accepts them, faults and all. And they generally respond to that person. Your job is not to judge the people on your team, but to help them—and let them help you— reach team goals.

The ability to deal with people is as purchasable a commodity as sugar or coffee. And I pay more for that ability than for any other under the sun.
                                      —John D. Rockefeller

ADAPTING YOUR BEHAVIOR

Once you've accepted your team, adapt your behavior to the needs of the individual. Learn what it takes to make each person on your team comfortable with you. If Missy seems more comfortable talking to you in a straight-backed, feet-on-the-floor position, follow her lead and sit up straight. If Bruno is more laid back, you can do that. Learn to adapt to your team, even in the little things. Rachel loves lists and memos. Give them to her. And go ahead—tell Slick his haircut looks great.

Getting to know the people you work with isn't the same as knowing about them. You may never know the names of their pets, but you should understand their strengths and weaknesses. (And if it's important to them, well darn it—learn the names of those pets!)

PUTTING IT ALL TOGETHER

Every day you have countless chances to use and develop your interpersonal skills. A one-on-one relationship with a friend can be hard enough. No matter how well you get along, you'll run into problems. You want to ice skate, and he wants to swim.

On a working team, you'll need your people skills more than ever. Not only do you have to get along

with these people, you have to work together and produce. With so many different personalities and opinions, even the smallest decisions come hard. You need
to learn how best to handle members of your team.

Here's an example of a petty but typical workplace
problem that can disrupt teamwork. You have only
been on the job for three weeks. Management is
recarpeting your offices, but it's up to you and two
coworkers to decide on the color. Quiet Tim, the person you get along with best in the office, asks you to
side with him and choose red. Aggressive Annie,
who's obviously on the fast track to success in the
corporation, is demanding green. What do you do?

Answer? As with most relationships, there is no
easy answer. If you have a strong preference and it
matters to you, then you probably should express
your opinion.

But if you're people-smart, there are several things
you'll do to *handle* each team member. For instance,
don't deal behind Annie's back. If she's as sharp as
you think she is, she'll know. And she won't forget.
She's not someone you want to antagonize. If she's
on the fast track, she's doing something right. You
can learn from her. Ask her why she thinks green is
the way to go. Listen (don't forget eye contact)

while she answers you. If you end up choosing red anyway, do it honestly. Tell her you understand her viewpoint, but tell her you're going to have to go red this time.

If your vote is green, be ready to explain why. If you're quiet, like Tim, explaining your decision might not be easy. But both parties need to understand your rationale. Ask Tim to explain his preference. He may need encouragement to say openly what he said privately. You may want to explain your choice to him privately and make sure he understands.

You might suggest the three of you agree on a blue carpet. Behind the best negotiations are people who are people-smart. (Chapter 6 deals with negotiations and compromises.)

Arguing the color of a carpet may sound stupid. But offices have gone to war over less.

THE PROFESSIONAL TEAM

Part of being people-smart is understanding the nature of a professional relationship. Your coworkers are not your buddies—not at work anyway. You are professionals working together to accomplish a goal. Be professional.

Part of being people-smart is understanding the nature of a professional relationship.

Nancy had worked at a city newspaper for six months, long enough to be horrified at Cam's (the newest employee) unprofessional mistake. "She and I were discussing a story when our chief features editor walked out of her office. Before I knew what happened, Cam hollered after her, 'Pick me up a salami sandwich, will ya?' The whole room fell silent. We're pretty informal. But you just don't ask the features editor to pick up your lunch."

If you want to make it as part of a professional team, dress, speak, and act professionally.

TEAM PRIVACY

Hopefully you will become part of a team that works. Your interpersonal skills will help you win friends and strengthen your team. But no matter how comfortable you feel with your teammates, you're not at home. Be careful what you bring with you from home. Work is not the place to spill your guts.

Laurie felt nervous her first week teaching at a private school. As she puts it, "When I get nervous, I can get a severe case of diarrhea of the mouth."

On her second day of school, Laurie ate lunch with one of the friendliest teachers. When the woman commented on Laurie's rings, Laurie started in on family stories. "This one is an heirloom my father gave me. My mother bought me this one when I was in college. And," Laurie continued, going for the funny bone, "this is the one my husband bought me our first year out of graduate school—the year he was rich and famous."

Laurie sensed immediately that her coworker's attitude toward her changed. But she didn't realize the impact of that heart-to-heart until her first teacher evaluation. The incident had been reported to the principal: "Laurie brags at lunch about all her jewelry and her rich family."

You're probably better off keeping your money situation to yourself. An executive in a Chicago firm said he loses confidence in workers who worry about their own finances. "I always figure they'll go to the highest bidder. I can't count on their loyalty."

You may well end up taking your services to the highest bidder. That's your privilege. But it's not people-smart to advertise it. Keep your personal financial affairs private.

There are formalities between the closest of friends.

—Japanese proverb

STUDY TO GET SMART

Good teams aren't possible if you can't get along with team members. Learn to study people. Your efforts will pay off. Strong interpersonal skills may keep your company from getting rid of you when they downsize. Working teams are highly esteemed because they bring profits. It's great to be goal oriented in the business world. But you'll never reach those goals unless you get people-smart.

EXERCISE

1. Run a test for yourself. Experiment on a particular group or class. Don't tell them what you're doing, but begin applying your people-smart skills. Figure out how to encourage each person in your class. See if you can make a difference in your individual relationships. After one week, analyze how your new attitude has affected the group or class or an individual.

2. For one day, write down your own "Translation Book" of body language. See how many gestures and signals you can detect.

3 CHAPTER THREE
GREAT EXPECTATIONS: THE TEAM'S DREAMS

On Mike's first day of work, he arrived downtown so early he had to park his car in darkness. As he opened the glass door to the 12-story office highrise, he couldn't stop his heart from pounding. He straightened his tie while he waited for the elevator. As he stepped off onto *his* floor, Mike thought, "This is it. All my dreams have been fulfilled."

Ten hours later Mike crowded into the stuffy elevator, loosened his tie, and thought, "That was the worst day of my life. I'll never make it." Mike's dream had turned into a nightmare.

Mike had expected the glitzy job his recruiter described. Etched in his mind were scenes from movies, meteoric rise to wealth and fame, starring Mike.

One of the first tasks you'll have managing your new career is to adjust your expectations.

GET REAL

The following questions were put to people in a variety of careers after they were newly hired, and then again, after a year or two on the job: 1. What were your top expectations when you joined your work team? What were your chief concerns? 2. At the end of the year, what were your expectations? What were your chief concerns?

One of the clearest signs of a successful job transition is the shift of expectations. In most cases, that shift moves away from the individual and toward the team as a whole.

Change your focus of expectations away from yourself and toward your team. Expect success for your team. Work for that. Get pride in the way your team works together and achieves goals.

FACTOID:

To see how your salary stacks up with others', check periodic salary survey results published by the Trade and Professional Association or contact your local chamber of commerce.

TOP EXPECTATIONS

New Workers	Workers After the First Year
Praise for getting to work on time	Learn from those on the team who have more experience
Praise for staying overtime	
Affirmation that I was doing a great job	Ask questions and take risks
A promotion by the end of the year	A fair evaluation if I fulfill my responsibilities
A raise after six months	
Bonus pay	Fair play and good working relationships with most people on my team
Coworkers who were my best friends	
A friendly relationship with my boss	Do a lot of things that aren't on my job description
Rave reviews on my first evaluation	
Recognition for my contribution	Work hard to keep this position
Understanding when I was late for a good reason	Respect if I can earn it and give it
Somebody to tell me what to do and how to do it	Join in the credit my team gets for accomplishing our goals

THE REAL WORLD

Guess what? As you step off that elevator and into your first job, you're not the only one with expectations. Your employers have their expectations too.

Interviews with over 20 personnel and team managers turned up the following expectations:

TEN TEAM EXPECTATIONS

1. Get to work on time (or early).
2. Put in more hours than required.
3. Learn from coworkers.
4. Be curious—ask questions of everyone on the team.
5. Master necessary skills.
6. Meet (or beat) deadlines.
7. Unselfish cooperation with the team.
8. Dress and act professionally.
9. Contribute to the fulfillment of team goals.
10. Be responsible and dependable— someone the team can count on.

A BRAVE NEW WORLD

Beginning a new job is a lot like moving to a foreign country. Don't be fooled if the people there look somewhat like you and your office computer is just like yours at home. It's a whole new world, with different customs and a culture you are going to have to figure out.

Figuring out a team's culture and customs isn't always easy. If you don't appreciate the fact that you're in a foreign land and have a lot to learn, you'll make your job that much harder. Missionaries and businesspeople who move to other countries often report that culture shock lasts longer in countries that are most like the United States. Why? Because an American may feel at home in London. The language and clothes are nearly identical to what she's used to. But the false sense of familiarity breeds discontent. She is *not* home. If she doesn't acknowledge the differences soon, she may never adjust.

The same is true in the business world. Learn to discern the culture and customs of your team.

LAWS OF THE LAND

You may be able to get your first ideas of team culture and customs before you show up for work. Read all

(V. Harlow/Russell Library)

When beginning a new job, learn as much as you can about your new company. For example, go to your local library to see if your employer has an Internet site. Or, search for news coverage about your company on the Internet.

you can about your company. Your employer may give you literature. Read it. Learn the mission statement. Get a feel for what's important there.

44

Go to the library and check out articles about your company. Try Internet search engines. Knowledge is power.

THE UNWRITTEN RULES

Most of what you need to know about your job, won't be found in writing. Once again, it's time to play detective. Observe how things work on your team. Ask questions. Take notes.

The following sections identify some things to look for.

Company Dress

It may not be stated in your company policy manual, but if everyone in your office is wearing a suit and tie, don't come to work in sweats. Take your cue from people who have worked there a long time. Be conservative when you start out. Don't let the way you dress detract from who you are and what you have to offer. Don't be the most dressy or least dressy in your department. And purple hair is probably out.

Level of Familiarity

When it comes to friendships with your teammates, follow their lead. Be friendly and professional to everyone, but don't force a friendship out of desperation or loneliness. Don't assume you'll be included right away. Let them invite you.

Some people don't kid around—ever. Don't be the loudest person at the lunch table. And save the locker-room jokes for another audience.

Don't assume that because your boss is friendly, you're her friend. Don't go to a first-name basis unless you're clearly told to do so.

Lee Wilkins, manager of human resources at Gorman-Rupp Company, laments the unprofessional behavior of many first-year employees. "Last month one of our interns, on her way out, hollered across the room, 'Hey, Lee! Wanna go with?' I said no. But what I felt like saying was, 'With what? I'm not your 'bud' and I have no intention of becoming one.'"

Use of Free Time

Watch what everybody else does during breaks. Some of your team members may use that time to work and catch up on things. Others need time alone. Just because you're used to socializing during breaks, don't drop in on them for a chat.

If everybody gathers at the water cooler after

lunch, don't be the odd one out. Observe and detect the culture and do all you can to fit in.

Unofficial Pecking Order

From flow charts and department titles, get familiar with the way authority runs in the office. But most workplaces have an underground pecking order. Observe which people command most respect. Where do people go when they want advice? Where do they go to get something done in a hurry?

Answers to these questions will help you decipher your team's culture.

Ecology

Many offices place great emphasis on recycling and conserving resources. Lisa was embarrassed when she had to be told by her boss that she was being wasteful. She realizes now that she should have noticed what her coworkers were doing for the environment. "I didn't even notice everybody else brought a glass mug for coffee. I just kept using up those styrofoam cups. I figured since a girl came in to clean up every night, I didn't have to clean up, too. But my coworkers always did." Lisa learned the hard way that office culture matters.

(Joe Duffy)

Unspoken Communication

All of us are watchers—of television, of time clocks, of traffic on the freeway—but few are observers. Everyone is looking, not many are seeing.

—**Peter Leschak**

Steve didn't see a sign forbidding his entrance to the elevator on the right. But as soon as he stepped in, he knew something was wrong. He had been standing with two coworkers, but neither of them followed him into the elevator. He looked at the four

48

people who shared the elevator with him, but none returned his smile.

Steve got off the elevator and waited for his co-workers. When he asked why they hadn't gotten on, one of them said, "That's the executive elevator, Steve." No signs, no instruction book, but company culture nonetheless.

Some customs can be detected if you practice reading people's expressions and body language. When you talk about your old friends and school, do people look away and excuse themselves? Pay attention to their reactions to topics of conversation. In some offices, political discussions are off-limits. Your dating life or your children or hobbies might not be welcome subjects to your team. Learn to read people so you'll know.

HIDDEN TRAPS TO AVOID

Do all you can to avoid these hidden traps and unwritten pitfalls:

- *Secret passages.* Take a wrong turn, ally yourself with the wrong person, and you step off the path of success.
- *Closed doors (even when open).* Just because your boss or teammate leaves the door open doesn't

49

mean you can read it as an invitation to walk in
whenever you feel like it.

- *Unmarked signals.* Miss the subtle body language
  of teammates, and you'll commit the same blun-
  ders over and over.
- *Misleading signs.* Your boss calls you by your first
  name, but don't drop your boss's Ms. or Mr. until
  you're invited to do so.
- *Silent bells.* In many businesses, "9 to 5" is just
  an expression. Get over your school bell mentality and expect to stay after school.

THE WAY THINGS ARE DONE

Ever sit with a small group of friends who hang out
together? When some "outsider" sits with you, the
atmosphere changes. This new person might talk
about things you don't usually talk about. Her slang
may be different and she misses the meaning of your
inside jokes. You have to explain everything and still
she doesn't seem to get it.

FACTOID:
SOP means "Standard Operating
Procedure"—the way (policies, regulations)
the company operates.

WHAT NOBODY TELLS YOU
(But You Better Know Anyway)

1. Don't talk back to the boss. He's not your prof, looking for a discussion.

2. Learn the ropes before you suggest a change.

3. Nobody succeeds by clockwatching.

4. Allow plenty of time in the morning for problems—traffic, snow, earthquakes, disasters. There's no such thing as a good excuse.

5. New ideas aren't necessarily better.

6. Don't talk about your old life, friends, or boss.

7. You don't necessarily have the same privileges as everybody else yet.

8. Your boss doesn't have to be tactful.

9. Your teammates aren't necessarily your buddies.

10. Don't dress strangely. Manage your own first impression.

11. Job recruiters are never around when you need them—and they exaggerate.

12. Your job description is just an outline.

That's you as the new kid on your team. John's father was in the military and moved his family with him for each new assignment. John knew what it was like being the new kid, and he used his skills at adapting when he started his own career. John talks about his transition to a printing company and his adjustment to his team. "I went to six schools in nine years and got pretty good at reading the way things worked at a school. After the first day, I knew which teachers would be easy, how to steer clear of the principal, which kids I should try to hang with. So when I started working at Bookman, I just did the same thing. I watched and I listened. It worked out."

Be a good detective as you figure out your team's culture. Then nobody will have to say those dreaded words: "That's not the way things are done around here."

If you're the new kid at school, you won't get far by coming in and trying to take over. Your job is to learn how to get along in the new setting.

The same goes for your career. Your first year is the time to accept your team and your team's culture, discern their customs and adapt. It won't be easy. Most of us spend years trying to find our individuality. You've been struggling to be your own person. Now,

EXAMPLES OF "THE WAY THINGS <u>ARE</u> DONE AROUND HERE"

1. Customers and clients are never told about in-house problems.
2. Information isn't withheld from teammates in order for an individual to look good.
3. We don't go over the boss's head.
4. We don't bother the supervisor with details.
5. Or, we do go over details with the supervisor before acting.
6. Executives don't eat (ride elevators, chat, etc.) with new hires.
7. Managers aren't contradicted or challenged by their teams when a boss is present.
8. Certain wild behavior at office parties is forbidden.
9. Nobody orders alcohol at lunch.
10. Never promise customers dates that can't be met.

in a way, it's time to be theirs. You've been hired by a company to become part of a team. You'll have time later to resurface and more fully express your individuality. But for now, adapt to the team's style and culture. Make their expectations your expectations.

EXERCISE

1. List at least five "unwritten rules" of the group you hang out with.

2. Pick one of your classes and imagine you're writing a manual entitled *The Way Things Are Done in This Class.* What would you be sure to include?

3. What are your top 10 expectations as you begin a career? Are any of them not quite realistic?

CHAPTER FOUR
WORLD CUP TEAMS

Today's business teams reflect the ethnic makeup of our country. Walk into most businesses and you will probably see men and women from various cultures, ethnic backgrounds, races, and even countries. Not everyone on your team will be someone you would have gravitated to naturally. And yet, you will need to work more closely with these people than with anyone else you know.

Even if your job includes only a few people fairly similar to you, you can count on the diversity of your customers. In the 21st century, nearly everyone will need to know how to get along with other cultures and races in the workplace. A "World Cup team" is a diverse group of people who know how to work together to win as a team.

A "World Cup team" is a diverse group of people who know how to work together to win as a team.

(Courtesy: Union Summer 1996)

When working with people from various cultures, it's important to accept them for who they are. The different cultural perspectives each person brings to the group can help you reach a common goal.

WHAT'S THE DIFFERENCE?

Depending on where you went to school, you may have a wealth of multicultural experiences to take with you to your new career. But don't assume that just because you went to school with people of other races and ethnic backgrounds, you're all set. Attending classes is one thing; working on a team is something else. Teamwork requires a depth of understanding and acceptance.

POTENTIAL DIFFERENCES IN TEAM MAKEUP

► Men and women
► Race
► Nationality
► Cultural Background
► Customs
► Religion
► Financial Status (haves and have-nots)
► Education
► Experience
► Level of Skill
► Age
► Marital Status
► Social Life (drinkers/nondrinkers; smokers/nonsmokers; partiers/nonpartiers)

Do you recognize some differences around you at school? Run an inventory on the students you spend most of your free time with. How diverse is your group? Does it reflect your school's diversity, or do you only travel in the circle of people who are most like you?

If you're keeping your distance from other races and cultures, you may need to rethink. Make an effort now to understand and interact with people who are different from you, and your effort will pay off—now and later. You'll be preparing for a world-class team.

DIFFERENT DOESN'T MEAN WRONG

What your employer wants is a team of people who, no matter how different as individuals, can work together. The first step toward working with diversity is to acknowledge differences. The next step is to accept those differences.

Don't expect to change people from other cultures. It's not your job to mold them to what you consider the correct way of doing things. Instead, expect to learn from others as they learn from you. They may do many things differently, but it doesn't mean they're wrong.

Every man I meet is my superior in some way.
In that, I learn from him.
                          —Ralph Waldo Emerson

Janelle and Ray worked for the same international company, but held positions in different branches. They ran into the same problem working in multicultural environments. But they handled their situations differently.

At work, the Japanese members on Janelle's team spoke to each other in Japanese, leaving Janelle to wonder what they were talking and laughing about. Because she felt uncomfortable around them, she spent her time developing relationships with the other Americans on her team. After a year, two factions—American and Japanese—had developed in their department. Their team failed to achieve yearly goals and had to restructure.

Ray felt the same discomfort on his team as Janelle felt on hers. But after a couple of weeks, he worked up the nerve to ask the Japanese workers if he could talk to them about something. He explains what happened. "I found out that they felt the same way I did, like the Americans were leaving them out. And there were more of us, too. One of the Japanese Americans said she felt uncomfortable talking in English because she was aware of her accent."

Ray says the Japanese workers continued to speak in Japanese with each other. But after the discussion, everybody made more of an effort to bridge the language barrier.

Hopefully, nonnative speakers will have the English language skills they need to do the work required and to develop team relationships. But unless they have to speak English to do the job, it's against the law to force them to converse in English. It's not your job to change them. Instead, be honest, be friendly, and respect their language.

Language may be the most obvious cultural difference. But it's just the beginning.

POTENTIAL CULTURAL DIFFERENCES

▶ Language

▶ Food

▶ Manners

▶ Holidays

▶ Physical mannerisms

▶ Concept of personal space (what's mine/yours/ours)

▶ Ethics

▶ Values

▶ Family

▶ Ownership

▶ Time

▶ Dress

Remember that the outward differences just show the tips of the iceberg. All you see is a coworker who won't work on Saturday. Another refuses to work on Sunday. But behind those outward differences lie deep-seated beliefs, values, attitudes, and expectations.

All your people skills need to come into play for intercultural team relationships. Eileen kept a notebook of observations when she was a foreign exchange student in France during her junior year of high school. Her habit of noticing, adapting and accepting people made Eileen's career transition easier.

Eileen, now a buyer for a large department store, explains: "My supervisor here thinks I can get along with anybody. For example, I've noticed which cultures like handshakes. With French clients, I extend my hand when we meet and when I leave. Other clients [from other countries] are more comfortable doing business after a huge lunch during which nobody talks business. I do what makes the client comfortable."

It is the individual who is not interested in his fellow men who has the greatest difficulties in life and provides the greatest injury to others. It is from among such individuals that all human failures spring.

—Alfred Adler, psychologist

GOAL ORIENTED VERSUS PEOPLE ORIENTED

One way to help us understand differences is to recognize how we look at success and identity. Although some Americans are more goal oriented and others people oriented, as a nation we tend to be goal oriented. Ours is a culture of "doing," rather than a culture of "being."

CHARACTERISTIC DIFFERENCES IN THE WAY WE THINK

Goal Oriented	People Oriented
Self-worth comes from achieving	Self-worth comes from relationships
Time is tightly scheduled	Time is relative
Individualism vital	Needs to belong
Future oriented	Bound to past
Needs change	Seeks stability
Immediate family important	Extended family vital
Likes measurable goals	Wants people to agree

(V. Harlow)

Certain characteristics are often shared by people with a common cultural background. For example, Americans, as individuals or when working as a team, tend to be more competitive and goal oriented than people from some other cultures.

What do you ask when you first meet someone? "Where do you go to school?" "What jobs have you had?" "What do you want to do when you graduate?"

Or are your questions more like these: "Tell me about your family." "Did you grow up around here?" "What's it like living where you live?"

The first set of questions are more goal oriented. What do you *do?* The second set centers on people. Who are you? If you met someone of Slavic descent, for example, you might get to know that person fairly well before you were asked about your job. Americans usually find the answer to the job question in the first five minutes.

Americans tend to be competitive. But in Africa, home of some of the greatest runners in the world, many people race for fun, waiting at the finish line so all can cross together.

You'll run across many cultural differences in your career. Learn from them. Different doesn't mean wrong.

PLAYING FAIR

Eileen, the buyer who spent a year as a foreign exchange student, says there's a trick to fair play in dealing with other cultures. She says, "I've never met anybody who didn't think they were meeting the other person halfway. But what looks like 50–50 to you never looks like 50–50 to the other guy." We have to go out of our way to help other people feel like part of the team.

FIVE TRICKS TO FAIR PLAY

1. Be a help, not a critic.

2. Don't expect someone from another culture to know all about yours. Try to learn all you can about theirs.

3. Don't jump to conclusions based on stereo-types. (That's why he's late. That's why she's emotional.)

4. Be alert for gender and culture concerns.

5. Build bridges of understanding and respect. (Your career may depend on it.)

It's not your job to change people or demand they change. Your job is to get along and respect your team.

An attitude of fair play doesn't think, "That guy doesn't even know that we don't do that kind of thing here." Instead, the difference is seen and accepted: "In his country (or neighborhood) that's one of the things people do." Remember, until you're the boss, it's not your job to change people or demand they change. Your job is to get along and respect your team.

(Joe Duffy)

SEXUAL HARASSMENT

Carl was the life of every party in high school. Girls were dying to go out with him. Carl knew enough not to tell flat-out dirty jokes at the office, but he was quick with the one-liner, the sexual innuendo that could make a girl blush. After two weeks, Carl was called into the personnel office. Two women had complained of sexual harassment.

What is sexual harassment? The law defines it as any unwelcome sexual advances or requests for sexual favors, or any conduct of a sexual nature when:

- Submission is made explicitly or implicitly a term or condition of initial or continued employment.
- Submission or rejection is used as a basis of working conditions including promotion, salary adjustment, assignment of work, or termination.
- Such conduct has the purpose or effect of substantially interfering with an individual's work environment or creates an intimidating, hostile, or offensive work environment.

Most companies try to come up with a clearer definition. Gorman-Rupp, an international manufacturing company expands the policy:

Sexual harassment is unlawful....All employees have the right to expect a workplace which is free of conduct that is of a harassing or abusive nature. Offensive employee behavior also includes physical advances or intimidations, sexual or otherwise, and uninvited suggestive remarks. Any employee who joins in or condones harassment or abuse of another employee shall also be liable for discipline.

Did you catch some of those phrases? *Uninvited suggestive remarks...any employee who joins in.* Work is not the place for Carl's innuendos. What you say and how you say it may be interpreted as suggestive.

You've heard about harassment cases filed against senators, business managers, professors, construction workers, and students. It's no joke. Whether or not someone files a suit against you, you will be hurting your team and wrecking your own career if you engage in such activity.

SEVEN WAYS TO AVOID SEXUAL HARASSMENT

1. Cut out crude jokes.

2. Don't laugh at crude jokes.

3. Be careful about teasing the opposite sex.

4. Watch the way you word compliments. ("That's an attractive dress" rather than "sexy dress.")

5. Don't repeatedly ask a coworker out.

6. Stick with "hi" and a handshake, rather than the hello or goodbye hug or kiss.

7. Don't repeatedly exclude the opposite sex from discussions and activities.

If, on the other hand, you are the victim of sexual harassment, don't put up with it. You don't have to. First, talk to the person or people involved and clearly tell them you consider their actions and attitude sexually harassing. Ask them to stop. If they don't, inform them that you are serious and plan to take your official complaint to the company, through channels. Then do it. If your boss won't take you seriously, see your company's representative or a good lawyer. Sexual harassment is against the law.

F A C T O I D :
The Equal Pay Act of 1963 requires equal pay (for men and women) for equal work.

PREPARING FOR THE MULTICULTURAL ENVIRONMENT

How can you get ready to function on your multicultural team? Take advantage of the opportunities around you. Take a foreign language. Find a pen pal in another country and try to learn about another culture. Get involved in an international club for high school or college students. Host or invite foreign students into your home for holidays or hospitality. Join a volunteer organization that serves other cultures.

Join a church or community groups that have out-reach programs.

Talk. Men and women have different points of view on many things. Try to understand. Ask questions.

If there's a student with a disability in your school, get to know her. If you feel awkward talking down to someone in a wheelchair, tell that person. Be honest. Honesty is the start of understanding and being understood.

Want to be on a World Cup team? Start now to broaden your understanding of the world. The more people you can get along with now, the smoother your transition is likely to be when you join your work team.

EXERCISE

Try some of these exercises to sharpen your point of view and help you see things from someone else's point of view.

1. Think of the last time you argued with someone. Write out the argument as if you're the other person. What are you (as this other person) trying to say? What are your thoughts when you're not being understood?

2. Imagine you're the opposite sex and someone has just made a sexual joke at your expense. Write down how you feel.

3. When's the last time you felt terribly out of place? Write down what it felt like. What made it worse? better?

4. Imagine you come from another racial background. How do you feel when you're around a group of laughing students of a different race?

5. List five things you've said or done this week that *could* have been called harassment.

CHAPTER FIVE
TEAM FIGHTS AND FRICTION

One widely used appraiser for new employees begins with these performance factors:

- Works effectively in groups.
- Resolves team conflicts.
- Works with other departments.
- Establishes and maintains cooperative working relationships.
- Is flexible and open-minded, focusing on team efforts.

No matter where you work, getting along with your coworkers, the members of your team, will be one of your most important duties. You can't just change "groups" or decide not to play. There's no semester break, no change of class and teacher. This is your team, and you better learn to get along.

PERSONALITY TYPES

Have you ever run up against someone who rubbed you the wrong way? You just couldn't seem to get along. Not your type, you decided. Although it's never a good idea to box people into convenient types, an understanding of basic personalities can help us appreciate where other people are coming from. If we can understand them, we may be able to avoid some personality conflicts.

One system of classifying personality types is according to temperaments. Four distinct temperaments, or personality types, were identified by Hippocrates over 2,000 years ago: sanguine, melancholy, choleric, and phlegmatic.

- *Sanguines* are fun, outgoing people who enjoy an audience and all the attention they can get. Their strengths usually lie in public speaking, being at ease with a variety of people and a readiness to risk and try new things.
- *Melancholies* are more introspective, deep thinkers. They tend to be artistic and are capable of deep friendships. They can be well organized and analytical.
- *Cholerics* are born leaders, and they know it. They are confident, usually goal-oriented and capable.

You can count on them to follow through with their plans and lead the charge to goals.

- *Phlegmatics* are easy-going and likeable. They seem to get along with everybody and keep themselves and life in balance. They can adjust well to most circumstances and people.

FOUR PERSONALITY TYPES

Sanguine
Outgoing
Popular
Life of the party
Live for fun

Melancholy
Artistic
Close friendships
Organized
Analytical

Choleric
Leader
Confident
Forceful
Goal oriented

Phlegmatic
Easygoing
Gets along with all
Well balanced
Steady

DEALING WITH DIFFERENT PERSONALITIES

Imagine that you spend a week observing the members of your team and conclude Sam is a sanguine; Mary, a melancholy; Carl, a choleric; and Farah, a phlegmatic. (Hopefully you won't put your teammates in such tight boxes. Few people fit 100% into a single personality type. So, just imagine, for the sake of illustration.) What conflicts should you watch out for? If you have an idea what to expect, you can *act, not react.* Also, what needs can you anticipate and help meet for each member?

Sam Sanguine

Sam Sanguine has been so friendly, you might think you'd never run into conflict with him. But remember, Sam needs to be the center of attention, the life of the party. Here are some potential conflicts you might have with Sam:

- If you are also a sanguine, you may represent competition to Sam. He'll resent it if you steal the spotlight. Jealousy and animosity could develop between you. If it happens, don't react. Let Sam have the applause. Just do your job.

- If you're not a sanguine, you may tire of Sam's need to entertain. Although you'll probably appreciate

The four temperaments named by Hippocrates are symbolized in these 1603 woodcuts done by C. Ripa. <u>Phlegmatics</u> (top left) have easy-going personalities and get along well with people; <u>Sanguines</u> (top right) are outgoing and enjoy being with the public; <u>Cholerics</u> (bottom left) are born leaders and goal-oriented; and <u>Melancholies</u> (bottom right are artistic, well-organized and serious thinkers.

the friendliness, you may be disappointed if you expect a deep friendship. Understand where Sam is coming from and accept the level of friendship he offers, even if it's not what you have in mind.

• Sam may not want to get serious when you're ready to get down to business. He'll infringe on your privacy, stopping by your desk for a chat while you're in the middle of an important project. Be careful how you explain your need to get on with your work.

What needs will Sam have? If you meet some of Sam's needs, you'll reduce the chances of personality conflicts.

• Sam needs your attention. It doesn't cost you anything, so go ahead and give it. Listen to Sam, and don't forget eye contact.

• Sam needs your approval. Compliment his ideas when you can. Laugh at his jokes, if they're not offensive. Be careful how you disagree with him.

• Sam may not realize it, but he could use help being consistent. He may drive your team crazy by showing up late for meetings or forgetting the agenda. Ask him if he'd like a copy of your notes. Remind him of meeting times. Offer to pick him up so he gets to an important conference on time. Minimizing conflict will help your team and it will help you.

Melancholy Mary

Melancholy Mary keeps up her end of your team's responsibilities. She's intense and always tries to do her best. So what kind of conflict could you run into with Mary?

- Because Mary tends to be a perfectionist, she will get upset if you're not orderly and disciplined, too. She's a perfectionist, and you're not perfect. Understand that her standards are high and that you may never do well enough to please her.

- Mary's perfectionism can make her negative. Act, don't react. She may find the downside to every team project. Don't get drawn into her negativism or depression.

- Mary is given to moodiness and sensitivity. You can easily hurt her feelings. Be sensitive, and don't joke at her expense. If you offend her, apologize. She can hold a grudge.

- Mary needs deep friendships. If you don't show an interest in things that are important to her, she may write you off as shallow or worse.

What needs could you try to help Mary fulfill?

- Mary needs to be drawn out. Ask her for her opinion. Talk to her about her interests.

- Do your best to meet her need for order and discipline. Don't be late for meetings. Keep schedules.
- Mary doesn't treat relationships lightly, and you shouldn't treat your relationship with her lightly either. Remember what things and people are important to her.
- Mary needs some time alone. Be sensitive to her desire to work rather than talk.
- Since Mary can get depressed, stay positive with her. Don't scold her, but encourage her by pointing out how well she's doing.

Carl Choleric

What about Carl Choleric? What conflicts could you run into with him?

- Carl honestly believes he's right and you're wrong. Arguing with him probably won't get you much more than a fight. Be diplomatic and don't buck his authority unless necessary.
- Carl expects you to work as hard as he does to reach goals. Work hard. Don't procrastinate. Follow through with your responsibilities.
- Understand that Carl is more focused on team goals than on team members. Don't be offended by his bark or his apparent lack of interest in you as

a person. Don't take his criticism personally. It's just his way.

Carl may seem so confident that he doesn't have any needs. But he does.

- Carl needs to succeed. Do all you can to make your team (and Carl) look good.
- Carl may step on team members' toes and not even know it. You may be able to follow along and smooth feathers from time to time, reminding others that Carl doesn't mean everything he says.
- On occasion, you might need to confront Carl. He can take it. He may not see your point of view, but you may need to try.

Farah Phlegmatic

Farah Phlegmatic is so easygoing, you may envy the way she seems to get along with everybody. But after a time, personality conflicts can surface.

- Farah is so easygoing, she can slip into laziness. When she doesn't do her part on a team project, you may resent her. Instead, accept her, but offer to help her meet her objectives.
- Farah is on such an even keel, she doesn't get too excited about anything. If you are excited, don't

be disappointed when she doesn't share your enthusiasm.

• Because Farah seeks peace above all else, she probably won't volunteer for extra duties or take risks for the team. You may get frustrated waiting for her to get off her duff and get going. Instead, think of ways you can challenge her to act.

How can you meet Farah's needs?

• Don't be argumentative with her. Help her keep the peace.

• When you see a job you're sure she'd be good for, encourage her to volunteer. Help her determine a plan of action.

• Understand that Farah may be hiding her problems. She'd rather live with dissatisfaction than risk a conflict. Be sensitive enough to figure out what Farah's hiding.

DREADED BEHAVIOR TYPES

Being aware of the different temperaments, or personality types, can reduce the number of team conflicts you get drawn into needlessly. But no matter how aware you are, there are certain behavior types you're bound to run into sooner or later. In fact, after you read about the four types (worst enemy, bum, child, tattletale), you'll probably think of people you already know who fit these descriptions. At school, you can usually just avoid these people. But if they're on your team, you'll need to know how to handle them. And, most importantly, never behave like one of these types yourself.

FOUR DREADED BEHAVIOR TYPES

Type	Defense Against
Worst Enemy	Keep records, send memos, confront
Bum	Offer to help, work hard yourself
Child	Offer alternate times for talk
Tattletale	Tell little about yourself

The greatest asset I possess, and the way to develop the best that is in a person, is by appreciation and encouragement.
**—Charles Schwab,
early 20th-century business leader**

(V. Harlow/Vinal Regional Vocational Technical School, Middletown, CT)

Whether you're at school or work, it's important to understand and accept your friends' different temperaments or personality types. This will enable you to work together as a team.

Your Worst Enemy

Your worst enemy on the job can take many forms: male, female, young, old, any personality type. She may want your job. He may want you to look bad. You may or may not have helped make this person your worst enemy.

Andrea had never had a worst enemy until she began working as a trainee for a telephone company.

It took her about three months to catch on. "This woman started by making fun of me to other trainees behind my back. I tried to laugh it off. But when I found out she'd told the supervisor I wasn't working out, I knew I had to do something to defend myself. The supervisor asked me how committed I was to my job, why I was late and left early. And it wasn't true."

Andrea's solution was to keep good records. "I told the supervisor I hadn't left early, but I didn't know if she believed me. From then on I kept detailed records on my calendar. I sent memos about projects. The next time I talked with my supervisor, I was armed."

Many worst enemies are deceivers. One approach is a direct confrontation. If you decide to confront, be specific. Don't blame. Instead of saying, "I think you're out to make me look bad," wait for a clear issue. "I was told by the supervisor that you reported I came in late last week. I have a record that in fact I came in early every day last week. I don't understand."

Memos to all team members, including your enemy, can make a good defense against accusations that you're not doing enough work. Make copies of everything you do.

Don't go over your enemy's head without informing him. Stay aboveboard so that none of the accu-

sations will have a foundation. Keep doing the right thing. Others will see it. Don't try to force your team to take sides or choose between you and your enemy.

The Bum

By now you've worked on enough group projects in school, in church, or some club to know there's bound to be someone on your team who doesn't carry his weight. What do you do when this happens on your team? How do you handle the bum who makes more work for you and everybody else because he doesn't keep up his end?

Megan hated group papers and projects in high school. "I always ended up doing the whole thing, or I got a lower grade because my partner didn't do her end." She didn't think she'd have an easy adjustment working on a team of librarians in a city library. After a week on the job, Megan recognized the same "bum" type in one of her team members. But she discovered her employers had a built-in way to handle the problem.

"We all signed a contract that included a team clause saying we were committed to working together as a team and sharing responsibilities and work. Our team leader had us come up with a list of things we expected from each other. One of the expectations was that everybody would do his share. So when Robert didn't, we all felt it. First, we asked him how we could help him make his commitment. We did his work for him sometimes, but we didn't cover for him. And after awhile, he was let go."

Usually, if you keep doing what you need to do, the bum won't last. Give him enough rope, and he'll hang himself.

The Child

The "child," also known as the "baby," hasn't grown up enough to act like a professional. She brings all her personal problems to the office and wants you and everybody else to take care of her. If you let her, she'll waste your work time telling you the sordid details of her love life. Her feelings are so easily hurt, you may be afraid to tell her you don't have time to talk.

How do you handle the needy child? If you tell her what you think straight-out, she probably can't handle it. You may make the conflict worse and affect your relationship with her and the functioning of your team. On the other hand, if you say nothing, she'll drain you.

Gretchen had a "child" on her shift in retail sales. Every free moment, the other woman latched on to

Gretchen to pour out her latest personal trauma. "I couldn't just tell her to stop talking to me," Gretchen said. "So I started offering her other times."

Gretchen tried to word her requests politely and warmly: "So we don't miss a customer, let's save our talk for the next break." Or, "I'd like to hear this, but I'm afraid I won't be able to focus. Would you like to go out to lunch Friday and tell me about it then?"

You have to be careful not to hurt a "child's" feelings, but you can't get drawn into being his therapist. Be the adult, the tactful adult.

The Tattletale

The tattletale loves to be the bearer of juicy news. He knows everything about everybody in the office, and he loves to spread the word. How do you handle the tattletale?

First, if the news he's spreading is about you, then you know not to tell him anything not for public broadcast. The less you tell him about yourself, the less ammunition he can have against you.

If he chooses to tattle or gossip to you about other people, be polite, but don't buy into the revelation. If you're not impressed or interested, he will probably not waste his time on you. If he continues, it's better to handle him with questions than to accuse. "And you saw her do that?" you ask innocently. Again, do the right thing yourself. Keep your personal life personal and refuse to gossip about others.

Pick Your Fights Carefully

Do all you can to avoid team conflicts through understanding and acting, rather than reacting. But if nothing short of direct confrontation works, be sure you pick your fights carefully.

> If nothing short of direct confrontation works, be sure you pick your fights carefully.

Employers don't put up with in-house fighting. For your own sake, save your complaints for the majors. Minor irritations aren't worth a fight. Be prepared to be patient, to give more than you receive, to do more than your fair share. Andrea endured a lot of snide remarks from her "worst enemy" before confronting her and involving the supervisor.

Here lies the body of William Jay,
  Who died maintaining his right of way—
He was right, dead right, as he sped along,
  But he's just as dead as if he were wrong.
                    from the *Boston Transcript*

Plan your "fights." Don't get drawn into one through anger or frustration. Present your case logically, rationally, and honestly. Keep the argument pointed to issues, rather than individuals. Try saying, "It didn't get done," rather than "You didn't do it."

Finally, whenever possible, give the other guy a way out, a way to save face. Winning an argument or a battle may feel good for a minute, but you're going to have to put up with a sore loser for a long time. Don't lose a relationship just to get your way on one issue.

Author Max Lucado says, "Conflict is inevitable, but combat is optional. Use your God-given creative energy to resolve conflict before it escalates into combat."

EXERCISE

1. What personality type or types do you think you are? Why?

2. Think of two people you have trouble getting along with. What personality types do you think they are? Write down three ways mentioned in this chapter that you might try to handle them.

3. Do you know any people who might fit the descriptions of the worst enemy, bum, child, or tattletale? What have you done to try to get along with them?

CHAPTER SIX
TEAM GOAL SETTING AND NEGOTIATING

Goals come in all sizes. Every day you set certain goals and try to meet them. Some you work hard for. Others are more like wishes.

On school mornings you probably have a goal to get to class on time. To reach your goal, you break the task down into bite-sized pieces, or objectives: get up, eat breakfast, dress, get to school.

Your goal is to make your entrance at 8:05. If you're superorganized, you set your alarm for 5:30 A.M. Next, you give yourself 20 minutes for breakfast. To reach that objective, you have a system: grab spoon and bowl in one hand, milk and cereal in the other.

You need 30 minutes in the bathroom. Experience tells you that you may run into trouble. Your sister also needs 30 minutes. Same bathroom. You have several contingency plans. Cut 5 minutes off breakfast. Turn off your sister's alarm. Or, just beat her in the mad dash down the hall to claim first dibs on the bathroom.

The rest of the morning has been broken down into dressing time and getting to school. Those objectives reached, you walk into school at 8:04. You reached your goal.

If you didn't set clear goals and objectives, the story has a different ending. Sure, you'd like to get to school on time. But you didn't think to set an alarm. Mom yells to wake you up, but you drift back to sleep. When you get to breakfast, you're too sleepy to know what time it is. And your sister won't appear from behind closed bathroom doors for hours. You wear the clothes you wore yesterday, but you're still too late to catch the bus. It's second period when you walk into class. And you're still not sure what made you late.

Goals and objectives are a part of everyday life. As a member of a professional team, you'll need to know how to participate in setting team goals. Those goals and objectives will determine everything your team does.

DEFINING THE MAIN GOAL

Most schools have the story, buried somewhere in a dark past. Billy Bob, pumped for his debut with the varsity football team, intercepts a pass, runs for all he's worth—and crosses the goal line, the wrong goal line. He reached the goal, but it was the wrong goal.

The first step in setting team goals is to define the main goal. Underlying any goals your team sets is the company goal. Your company will have a statement of purpose or a mission statement. Make sure you understand what it says, and what it doesn't.

John's first job was selling retail in a hardware store. He assumed that his employer's main goal was to sell more products and make more money. So John pressed every sale, making sure most customers left with something. But the hardware store relied on returning, faithful clientele. John's customers left with purchases, but some of the customers never returned. And John got called into the boss's office.

After you read your employer's mission statement, talk to team members. Ask them what they think are the unstated goals of the organization. The goals your team sets have to align with the company's stated and unstated goals.

CLEARLY STATE THE GOAL

When Gorman-Rupp, a major pump manufacturer, asked departments to come up with their own goals, one department started with this: "To increase production of parts." That goal wasn't accepted. Why not? It fit perfectly with the stated and unstated goals of Gorman-Rupp. So why wouldn't increased production of parts make a good goal?

Visualize the goal. If you can't, then your goal isn't clear.

A good goal has to be specific, measurable. How would the team know exactly when they met their goal? When they produced one more part than current rate? And how long did they have to meet the goal? The final, acceptable goal clearly stated: "To increase production of parts from 23 to 30 by November 1." The team added a specific time and number to the goal.

Visualize the goal. If you can't, then your goal isn't clear. What will the achievement of your goal look like? Is your goal to raise money for CARE, or to get food to Africa? The answer affects your team's strategy. Will you only try to get cash contributions, or will you go for donations of food? Do you need to plan how to convert your cash into food? You won't know unless your goal is clearly stated. Get it in writing. The clearer the vision of where you're going, the easier it will be to get there.

(V. Harlow/Vinal Regional Vocational Technical School, Middletown, CT)

At a group meeting, all individuals should make positive comments that contribute to achieving the common goal.

If you fail to plan, you plan to fail.

—Anonymous

INVOLVE THE WHOLE TEAM

A strong team makes sure every member has a chance to help form goals. The trend in business is to empower teams with more authority. The logic is simple. The more involved you are in forming a goal, the more you have at stake to see it fulfilled.

95

First, take personal responsibility for your team's goals. Be prepared to contribute in meetings. Make positive suggestions, rather than shooting down other people's ideas. It's like your literature class. If you do your homework and reading, you'll have something to add to discussions. If not, you can just make fun of what other people say. And that's not much help.

Next, take responsibility for making your team pull together. (It's something every team member should do—even rookies.) If one team member is shy, ask for his opinion. If he has a good idea, say so. If he's easier to talk with one-on-one, talk to him first. Then in the meeting, you can help get him started: "Larry had a good idea about that."

Do whatever it takes to get the most out of your teammates...and out of yourself.

BREAK THE GOAL INTO OBJECTIVES

Once the team has a clear goal, it's time to divide that goal into smaller goals or objectives. If each bite-sized objective is achieved, the main goal should be reached.

At the University of Missouri, a group of six students set a common goal: to get pass/fail classes at the university by the beginning of fall enrollment. The goal was thoroughly discussed, then written clearly. They called themselves STEP (Student Team for Educational Progress).

The next step was to come up with bite-sized goals or objectives that would lead to the main goal. Students met for a brainstorming session and came up with over 70 possible strategies to get pass/fail classes on campus. Many of the brainstorming ideas were impractical or silly (stage a sit-in at Jesse Hall, deliver brownies to the trustees, kidnap...). But several ideas won a consensus of support. They could get students to sign a petition. They needed to research other universities that used a pass/fail system. A campaign would be created to make STEP seem like an organization of 600 students, rather than six. A dialogue would be set up with administrators.

The jobs were described and given a deadline for completion. Then each job was assigned to a particular group member.

F A C T O I D :

Everybody today is talking about empowerment. It means giving employees power or authority to make decisions only bosses used to make.

DIVIDE AND CONQUER

Once your team lists objectives and thoroughly discusses each one, it's time to divide the work. At the University of Missouri, one STEP member was an art student. She volunteered to head the publicity campaign. Another student felt comfortable speaking, so he volunteered to talk with administrators. Each member took on tasks according to his or her strengths.

As your team divides labor, volunteer for things you feel more confident about. Offer to do extra legwork, to help other members whose schedules may be fuller. Don't pretend with your team, or claim strengths you don't have. But if you are given tough jobs, go ahead and do your best.

COUNT ON TROUBLE

Assume that the other team members are giving their best, even if it doesn't look that way.

The time to anticipate problems is before you start. Brainstorm disasters. Ask what could possibly go wrong. Devise counterplans, contingencies. You have to be ready to react to the unforeseen.

As you head out in different directions, plan to meet regularly as a team. Give updates. Adjust as you go along. Assume that the other team members are giving their best, even if it doesn't look that way.

Then ask how you can help someone who isn't getting the job done.

The STEP team thought they might run into opposition from the faculty. To head that off, they conducted a survey of faculty and shared the results. They held a faculty forum to help change opinions. What they hadn't anticipated was opposition from students. A large group of students opposed the system. STEP had to make on-the-spot changes in their campaign.

No team can anticipate all the obstacles. But if you anticipate some, you can flex with the rest.

SECRETS TO TEAM GOAL SETTING

1. Each member takes personal responsibility for goals.

2. Every member needs to voice an opinion.

3. Each opinion (no matter how far out) should be weighed and considered carefully.

4. Team members volunteer to handle objectives that suit their abilities and strengths.

5. Members keep individual commitments.

6. Team members help each other achieve objectives.

7. The team shares the victory (or the blame).

TEAM CONSENSUS AND NEGOTIATIONS

It's not easy convincing one person to go along with your plan. So how can you get your whole team to agree with you? You don't. You work with your team toward a consensus, an agreement all of you can live with. You negotiate.

Negotiation isn't something new for you. You do it every day.

"Come home right after school," says Mom.

"Mom, I promised to meet Ken after school. Is six o'clock okay?"

"Supper's at 5:30. How about home at 4:30?"

"Five?"

"All right. Five, but don't be late."

"Thanks."

And your negotiation is successfully completed. At school on Wednesday, you ask your speech teacher to let you give your presentation last—on Monday. She had you scheduled for today, but lets you off the hook until Friday. You agree. That night you ask your dad for the car. And negotiations start all over again.

You negotiate all day. You don't argue until you get your way. Instead, you work toward a solution both sides can live with.

Teamwork requires constant negotiation. As your

team makes goals and sets strategies to achieve those goals, you'll have to come together and build a consensus. The result should be something each member can support—not one strong person's idea, not a majority. Your team needs a consensus.

FOUR STAGES OF TEAM DEVELOPMENT

Most work teams go through a transition on their way to becoming effective. The process usually moves through four stages: on guard, duel, healing, and victory.

The On-guard Stage

In the first stage, team members are "on guard." They have just formed a new team. Politeness reigns. No one wants to step on anybody's toes or look stupid. There's little overt friction or conflict, but there's little creativity either. Since irritations aren't expressed openly, resentment can build up. The on-guard phase may look like a success because team members are agreeing so easily, but don't be fooled. If your team never progresses beyond this polite beginning, you'll never function as a strong team.

What can you do to help move out of the on-guard stage? Don't sacrifice politeness, but feel free to ask sincere questions. Say, "I don't understand how that would work." Be brave enough to make other suggestions. "What do you think about...?"

Defer to experience, but know that one of your offbeat ideas you're afraid to share might be just what your team needs.

BARRIERS TO TEAM NEGOTIATIONS

Failure to listen

Fear of losing face

Pride

Fear of looking foolish

Failure to take personal responsibility
   for outcome

The Duel Stage

The second stage can turn into a duel. Most people can hold back resentment only so long. Something has to give. In the duel stage, tempers flare. The team divides over an issue, forming warring factions, each side resolving never to give an inch. Discussions move from controlled, short talks to shouting matches. The team gets nowhere.

The second stage is where many teams dissolve and quit trying. They know that they can work more effectively on their own. Why bother with this group of contrary people? It's not worth the effort.

But, if people can understand the process of coming together as a team, they can move through the dueling stage and discover what teamwork is supposed to look like. How can you help your team develop to the next stage? First, try to find a couple of positive points in the stances taken by each faction. Then, try to come up with an alternative. When arguments divide your team, no faction will win support. A new idea has to be found. If you can do that, you'll be on your way to the next stage.

GREAT THINGS TO SAY IN TEAM MEETINGS

"That's a good point."

"I see what you mean."

"I hear what you're saying."

"Good job."

"Well done. Nice work."

"Good idea."

"Hmmmm. That's interesting."

The Healing Stage

In the healing stage, team members settle down and ease into a routine of compromise. Ideas are exchanged. People start to listen and learn from each other, rather than trying to win others over. Team members devise their own ways of getting to a compromise, for example, a 10-minute limit on discussion. And for the first time, the team begins to see that the group can be more effective than the same individuals working independently. In the healing stage, teams begin to develop a sense of timing.

"TIMES" IN TEAM NEGOTIATIONS

A time to listen—even to ideas you don't like.

A time to speak—bite your tongue when it's not your turn.

A time to mediate—focus, clear up misunderstanding.

A time to learn—and see the other side.

A time to compromise—and find an alternative.

A time to accept—and change.

A time to support—and grow.

The Victory Stage

If the team hangs in there, healing will come—healing that leads to victory. And that's when teamwork begins to pay off bigtime. A mutual respect frees team members to take risks. Every idea gets expressed, so the team can glean out the best elements and put together the best possible plan.

One high school academic team felt they reached the victory stage by working on competitions and fund-raising projects. Some of their comments were: "When we were finished [raising money for new equipment], I couldn't even tell you who had done what. We had all accomplished what we wanted, and that was what mattered."

"Everybody worked as hard as they could. So even though some of us may have looked like we did more, our team knew the credit belonged to everybody."

"I didn't like the project we decided on, selling mums at homecoming. But I respected my teammates and threw myself into supporting the idea just as if I'd come up with it myself. I still don't think it was the best plan, but that didn't matter once we'd settled on it."

That team had reached the highest teamwork phase, the victory stage. And their teamwork paid off.

EXERCISE

1. Pretend you're on a committee of students who want to do away with all grades at your high school. What's your plan? List three goals and three to five objectives under each.

2. Imagine you are trying to bring two friends to a consensus. They disagree on where you should eat. One wants Dairy Queen, and the other wants Taco Bell.

3. List the four stages of team development. Next to each stage, jot the name of a group or team you think fits.

CHAPTER SEVEN
7 IT'S UP TO YOU

You'll be surprised at the influence you can have on your team, even as a rookie. You can encourage your team and spur them to success, or you can tear down team unity with proven team killers. It's up to you.

TEAM KILLERS

The 10 leading team killers are:

- Gossip
- Jealousy
- Prejudice
- Critical Spirit
- Selfishness
- Laziness
- Stubbornness
- Negativism
- Blame
- Deceit

Gossip

Robin works with a medical team in a hospital in the Northeast. She says, "Gossip can hurt our team like no other disease. Hospitals are notorious grapevines

(Joe Duffy)

"I'd watch what I say around him…He's a bit of a gossip."

of gossip. And it hurts our relationships. You get so you're afraid to say anything."

Gossip is destructive, and there's no room for it on a working team.

I will speak ill of no man and speak all the good I know of everybody.
—Ben Franklin

One solution to team gossip is to keep your complaints and criticisms on a "need-to-know" basis. Does the person you're talking to need to know this information about a third party? Is that juicy tidbit about your boss something your team needs to hear?

If the information is something you think your team or supervisor should know, be sure of your facts. Don't pass along someone else's gossip.

Next, to avoid being the subject of gossip, keep your personal life to yourself. Separate your professional life from your personal life. Don't give the gossipmongers ammunition with pieces of your love life or failures. Don't talk about how broke, bored, or unhappy you are.

The most effective solution to put a stop to team gossip is to practice *good gossip*. Make a point to pass along positive information to team members. If you're with Bill when he comments that Rhonda is doing a great job with the Hansen account, tell Rhonda the next time you see her. If the boss tells you she wants you to write a report like Bill's because Bill knows what he's doing, be sure to tell Bill the positive thing the boss said about him.

Compliments delivered by a third party are the most valued of all because we know they're sincere. Rhonda wasn't even around when Bill paid her the compliment. He wasn't flattering her or trying to be nice. So if you pass along that comment, that good gossip, to Rhonda, you'll exert a powerful influence for good. Good gossip can transform an office.

Jealousy

Team jealousy usually springs from individual insecurities. Unhealthy competition develops among team members. One person withholds helpful information from another. Nobody offers to help with tasks not directly in the job description. The result is a team that operates like competitors.

What can you do? First, don't be pulled into jealous competition with your teammates. Offer to help them succeed. Don't compare yourself with your teammates. Instead, know that you're doing your best. Suggest to your team that you all turn the competition outward. Compete with your business competitors.

When we have a brilliant idea, instead of making others think it is ours, why not let them cook and stir the idea themselves. They will then regard it as their own....
                                    —William Winter

Prejudice

Your team won't stand a chance if you tolerate prejudice in any form. Some business teams have an unofficial "old boys' club." No women allowed. Other teams divide along racial or cultural lines.

As a rookie, your best chance to influence your team is in your personal relationships with teammates. Try to develop solid relationships with everyone on your team. Be careful of subtle prejudices, choosing your friends by personality, or how much they're like you.

Beware of silent complicity. Don't be afraid to speak up when you see prejudice going on. And never laugh at cruel jokes or racial comments.

A DOZEN THINGS YOU SHOULD NEVER SAY TO YOUR TEAM

"Nobody told me."

"I didn't have time."

"That's not part of my job."

"No fair. He got to do it."

"But it's not my turn."

"Why do I have to?"

"She said that he said that you..."

"Well, it's not my problem."

"It's all your fault."

"He's the problem."

"I guess I forgot."

"I told you so."

111

Critical Spirit

It doesn't take great creativity to notice faults in other people. If you bring a critical spirit to your team, you can dampen enthusiasm and impede success. Don't be quick to point out flaws in the company or in the way your team conducts business. Don't waste your time criticizing other people.

Any fool can criticize, condemn, and complain—and most fools do.
—Dale Carnegie

It doesn't hurt you to believe the best of people. If Mary says she tried her hardest but couldn't get her part done in time, you might as well believe her and offer to help. Better to believe the best than assume the worst.

Another way to fight the team-killing, critical spirit is to "catch people being good." Some people lie in wait, hoping to catch others making mistakes. Instead, be on the alert for good things people do. Catch them being good and praise them for it—directly and to others. "Did you see the way Bill handled himself in that meeting? He knew just what to say." "Bill, I appreciated the way you drew Sam out in the briefing." Praise loudly; criticize softly.

Selfishness

From the moment you join a team, you need to shift gears. Your success now depends on how well your team performs—*not* on how good you look.

Selfishness makes you volunteer for the showy jobs or the tasks that don't require as much time or energy. Selfishness keeps you from sharing information that would help someone else.

The answer to selfishness is generosity. Look for ways to help your team. Remember, your own success depends on their success. Do more than your share.

Laziness

Laziness will kill a team. The old saying about a chain only as strong as its weakest link applies to teamwork. If you don't do your part, the whole team fails. This isn't high school, where you might get an extension or talk a teacher into letting you off. You can't cram the night before or copy someone else's work. You have to work...hard. And you won't be praised for it. It's expected.

Some teams form a contract of commitment: *I agree to show up on time or early. I'll contribute to discussions.* And so on. If your team has no such contract, make one with yourself. Write down your commitments to your team, and keep those commitments.

Laziness includes showing up late, leaving early, wasting time, procrastinating, failing to do what you say you will. If you bring laziness to your team, you not only kill your team—you just may lose your job.

Stubbornness

Part of a good team spirit is the spirit of compromise. Be a learner on your team. Don't come to meetings with your mind all made up. Stubbornness and inflexibility will kill your team. Your job isn't to win everyone over to your way of thinking. You need to move with your team toward a consensus, a solution you can all agree on.

Take on the role of mediator. In meetings, jot down what people say. When agreement is reached, get it in writing. Then, when arguments erupt, you can refer to your notes and get your team back on track.

Negativism

Your team may come up with goals and plans you don't think will work. Still, don't bring negativism to your team. Don't be the one who always says, "That won't work." If you have doubts, ask questions. "What would happen if...?" "Would it be better to...?"

Focus on the positives. No matter how wild the idea, you can probably find something positive about it. And if you can't, you still don't have to pour water on it. Wait and see.

Bring solutions to your team, rather than problems. If you can't get your part of the plan to work, don't drag into your team meeting, complaining, "It just won't work." Show up with an alternative plan, or at least a couple of ideas. And focus on the positives. The same difficulty can be viewed as a disaster or a challenge. It's all in how you look at it.

Bring solutions to your team, rather than problems.

Blame

When something doesn't work out right with your team project, resist the urge to blame someone. Don't ask who. Ask why? It doesn't matter whose fault it is. But if you can help discover why the problem occurred, you can help your team avoid it next time.

First, make sure you don't blame. Next, disarm others who are looking for a scapegoat. Keep your team on the positive track. *"Why* did this happen?" (not "Who did it?") and "How can we fix it?

115

Deceit

Deceit will kill your team and your relationships. Always be honest with your teammates. Of course you don't have to (or want to) tell them everything. But what you do tell them should be true.

Don't pretend to understand something you don't. Don't try to bluff your way through. Instead, ask questions and learn. You can't fool everybody anyway. Besides, it's better to tell the truth. That way you don't have to remember so much.

Most of the team killers thrive when you put yourself ahead of your team. But becoming a part of a team means putting team success ahead of your own.

Centuries ago a man named Ptolemy came up with a system to explain the world. He decided our planet was the center of the universe. "The moon, sun, planets, and stars revolved around the Earth," said Ptolemy. And his ideas were accepted as truth for thousands of years. But eventually his theory broke down. Copernicus proved that the Earth was not the center of the universe. The Earth revolved around the sun, just as the other planets did.

You may (or may not) have survived for years as the center of your universe. Look out for number one. Be your own person. Do it your way. Well, you aren't the center anymore. You're part of a team. Welcome to the universe.

"V-I-C-T-O-R-Y!"

Join the ranks of professionals who have found personal victory through teamwork:

▶ "We look for people who know how to work on a team. When you get people who know how to help and be helped, who understand that if the company folds, they fold too—then your company is going to succeed."

—Al Hershberger, national sales manager, Custer Products Incorporated

▶ "Small groups are, quite simply, the basic organizational building blocks of excellent companies."

—*In Search of Fxcellence: Lessons from America's Best-Run Companies,* Thomas J. Peters and Robert H. Waterman Jr.

▶ Bill Hewlett, founder of Hewlett-Packard, explains his company's victory: "There is a feeling that everyone is part of a team, and that team is H. P. It exists because people have seen that it works, and they believe that this feeling makes H. P. what it is."

—*In Search of Excellence*

(© Disney Enterprises, Inc.)

Being part of a team means commitment along with hard work. Walt Disney credited his successes to the team efforts of his organization

▶ In its height of success, Delta Airlines talked of victory in the airline industry: "There is a special relationship between Delta and its personnel that is rarely found in any firm, generating a team spirit that is evident in the individual's cooperative attitude toward others, cheerful outlook toward life and pride in a job well done."
—*In Search of Excellence*

▶ Walt Disney built an empire that still employs thousands and entertains millions. He said, "Everything here at Disneyland and the Studio is a team effort. I credit the success of my films to the teamwork in my organization."

—*Walt Disney: Famous Quotes*

Interviews with students reveal the same kinds of victory through teamwork. It's going on in communities and school settings all across America. Here's just a sample of what students say about teams:

▶ "This year we learned that decisions had to be accepted by the whole group. Then we all felt part of whatever came out of it."

—Senior High Youth Group

▶ "Everybody gave up time, energy, talents, abilities, without claiming to do more than his fair share. There were no fair shares. We all did everything we could for the team."

—Student Council committee

▶ "Our first promise to each other was to say 'yes' more often than 'no.' We grew to be committed to the team."

—Production committee for a theater group

▶ "We know each other so well that we use everybody's strengths, without feeling bad about our personal weaknesses. We know we could never get done the things we do if we just worked on our own."

—TNT (Top Notch Teens)

Develop a team mentality now. Volunteer for group projects in your community, church, school, and family. Practice your team skills and become a team player. Few skills will matter more as you launch your career.

GLOSSARY

Adapting behavior. Adjusting and modifying the way one acts in order to fit in.

Choleric. One of the four temperaments: confident, usually goal oriented, and capable.

Company culture. The customs, ways and procedures of a company and its way of doing business.

Consensus. General agreement of opinion.

Duel stage. The second stage in team development; initial politeness gives way to anger and factions, with each side resolving never to give an inch.

Goal oriented. Motivated by the achievement of goals and objectives.

Healing stage. The third stage of team development; team members settle down and ease into a routine of compromise, exchanging ideas and learning from each other.

Interpersonal skills. Knowledge and ability to get along well with people; tools to help build personal relationships.

Learning style. Individual's preferred method for acquiring information.

Melancholy. One of the four temperaments: artistic, usually organized and analytical, sensitive.

Mentor. An unofficial teacher, coach, advisor.

On-guard stage. The first stage in team development; team members remain polite and cautious, reluctant to voice dissenting opinions.

People oriented. Motivated by relationships and the desire for everyone to get along and do well.

People-smart. The ability to figure out what others need and want, and to handle personal relationships successfully.

Phlegmatic. One of the four temperaments: generally easygoing, well balanced, steady.

Sanguine. One of the four temperaments: outgoing, life of the party, popular.

Teamwork. The process of a group of people pooling their resources and skills to work together and achieve a common goal.

Temperament. One's nature, or customary frame of mind and natural disposition.

Victory stage. The fourth and final stage of team development; the group has achieved unity and accomplishes more than they would as individuals.

BIBLIOGRAPHY

Books

Bredin, Alice. *The Virtual Office Survival Handbook.* New York: John Wiley & Sons, Inc., 1996.

Capozzi, John M. *Why Climb the Corporate Ladder When You Can Take the Elevator? 500 Secrets for Success in Business.* New York: Villard Books, 1994.

Fuller, George. *The Workplace Survival Guide: Tools, Tips and Techniques for Succeeding on the Job.* Englewood Cliffs, NJ: Prentice Hall, 1996.

Kinlaw, Dennis C. *Developing Superior Work Teams.* Lexington, Mass.: Lexington Books, D.C. Heath and Company, 1991.

Pell, Arthur R. *Complete Idiot's Guide to Managing People.* New York: Alpha Books, Macmillan, 1995.

Peters, Thomas J. and Robert H. Waterman Jr. *In Search of Excellence: Lessons from America's Best-Run Companies.* New York: Harper & Row, 1982.

Vance, Sandra S. and Roy V. Scott. *Wal-Mart: A History of Sam Walton's Retail Phenomenon.* New York: Twayne Publishers, 1994.

Vilas, Donna and Sandy Vilas. *Power Networking: 55 Secrets for Personal and Professional Success.* Austin: Mountain Harbour Publications, 1991.

Wainwright, Gordon. *Essential Personal Skills for Life & Work.* San Diego: Pfeiffer & Company, 1993.

Internent

"Teamwork," Blaire,
http://www.doorway.com/ei/html/team/html

"Laying Foundations for Effective Teamwork," Blaire,
http://www.ee.ed.ac.uk./~gerard/Teaching/art0.html